THE ULTIMATE OTHER

Divorced. Woman. Jew.

THE ULTIMATE OTHER

Divorced. Woman. Jew.

Dr Jackie King

GRAMMAR
FACTORY
— EST. 2013 —

Published by Grammar Factory Publishing, an imprint of MacMillan Company Limited.

Grammar Factory Publishing
MacMillan Company Limited
25 Telegram Mews, 39th Floor, Suite 3906
Toronto, Ontario, Canada
M5V 3Z1

www.grammarfactory.com

King, Jackie
The Ultimate Other: Woman. Divorced. Jew.

Paperback ISBN 978-1-998756-96-4
eBook ISBN 978-1-998756-97-1

1. SEL016000 SELF-HELP / Personal Growth / Happiness. 2. FAM015000 FAMILY & RELATIONSHIPS / Divorce & Separation. 3. SEL027000 SELF-HELP / Personal Growth / Success.

Production Credits
Cover design by Designerbility
Interior layout design by Ashley Howell
Book production and editorial services by Grammar Factory Publishing

Grammar Factory's Carbon Neutral Publishing Commitment
Grammar Factory Publishing is proud to be neutralizing the carbon footprint of all printed copies of its authors' books printed by or ordered directly through Grammar Factory or its affiliated companies through the purchase of Gold Standard-Certified International Offsets.

CONTENTS

ACKNOWLEDGEMENTS

This book has been almost twenty years in the making. The process of writing provided my therapy, my reflection and my growth over that time. I can't say I ever thought my life would be as it is, but discovering the tools I have used to give my life meaning, purpose and a strong narrative has been one of the most rewarding journeys I have experienced. After almost completing the manuscript, and in the context of rising antisemitism, I decided to add another lens. That of identity politics beyond gender. This was an important part of my ongoing process of self-actualisation.

To Debby and Miriam for their patience and their contributions, reviewing multiple drafts with kindness and honesty. To my parents, Margy and Aby, for understanding that in writing this book I was being brave. And of course, to my children – who have held the biggest mirror to me and forced me to take account of myself in our most challenging times. Thank you. Mothering you has been the privilege of my life.

To those who read this book, our world is a scary place right now. For women, and Jewish women in particular, gender equality is still a long-term goal. Jewish women's voices need to be heard, their experiences acknowledged, their stories written. This is more important now than ever. I hope this book goes some way to progressing a conversation, which started for me with Project Deborah in 2014, about the role of Jewish women at home, in their communities, nationally and internationally, as well as a much longer and larger conversation about social cohesion and inclusion. A conversation about designing our own futures where we feel safe, validated and equal. A conversation about pride, advocacy, identity and belonging. About being different and vulnerable in otherness and having the strength to lead our own futures and narratives.

PREFACE

While this book reflects my own journey and focuses on my own identities, it is intended to help all women, regardless of background and identity. More unites us than makes us different – the experiences of being burnt out, stretched, alone, undervalued, and looking to make a change. This book is for women who are smart, ambitious and authentic. It is for women whose lives are so complicated and burdensome that they have lost themselves. They have lost their identity, their heart, their creative essence, their purpose, their meaning in trying to be everything to everyone. They have lost themselves in their attempt to be valued, deserving, acknowledged and recognised. It is for women who have left their jobs, marriages or communities to try to find themselves again. It is for women who want to emerge more independent, vulnerable, and comfortable with who they are, where they came from and who they want to be.

This book offers the process of 'design thinking' – empathise, define, ideate, prototype, test and launch – as a method of understanding internal, often conflicting, narratives and identities. In this book I have used design thinking to understand myself, in all my complexities. Woman. Divorced. Jew. Israeli. Mother. Daughter. Partner. Friend. Professional. Other. Design thinking is a process that can be used by all of us.

Identity politics, in particular notions of otherness, have been central to my identity. My sense of otherness has been with me for my whole life. I had often described myself as never fitting in. Different. Not my full self. I have always felt different because of a particular combination and intersectionality of my multiple identities. I have tried to use this to give voice to others, to advocate, to add diversity of thought to all that I am involved with. This book reflects this otherness – in fact it is its central tenet. Although I had studied identity politics at university, I wasn't really aware that I was living it, until I heard the phrase 'the Ultimate Other' in an online course on antisemitism through Yad Vashem, the Holocaust Museum in Israel. I realised this was the essence of how I felt about myself; a new moment of self-actualisation.

I hope that my learnings will support you or your loved ones to better develop the empathy required to understand yourself and those around you, articulate the complexities of your identity, and heal from trauma. The therapeutic value of the writing process and the creation of stories and narratives that help define us has been hugely important in my journey.

My hope in writing this book, with its many iterations and versions, is that my journey of reconciling my different identities – the many parts of myself, my past and my potential, my heart and my brain, my life's meaning, and my life's work – has a universal message.

I hope that it allows readers, and women in particular, to reflect on their own journeys and to share their vulnerability with self-compassion. There is no failure in this book, only writing, learning, re-writing, re-testing, and defining *my own* vision of success. At the end of the day, that is the only one that matters.

A WORK IN PROGRESS

I began writing this book in 2010. I had a six-year-old, a four-year-old and a newborn. But my marriage was essentially over. Swine flu, the Haiti earthquake, the Apple iPad and WikiLeaks were the news of the year. *American Idol, The Big Bang Theory, Downton Abbey* and a plethora of new reality shows were hitting our TV screens. But I was oblivious to these things at the time. I was thirty-four years old and trapped. I couldn't breathe. I couldn't sleep. I had no memory. I was a working mother of three children, lonely in my marriage, employed at a job below my capability, financially dependent, experiencing poor relationships across every part of my life and constantly feeling overwhelmed. I felt invisible and unvalued, immersed in the toxic practice of trying to meet the demands and expectations of everyone in my life. I walked around with large black bags under my eyes, feeling like a rubber band – stretched in every direction – with no nourishment or time to be. It was a shocking combination of exhaustion, burnout, stress, unhappiness and unfulfillment. I lived as a shadow of myself.

I was in 'fight or flight' mode all of the time, constantly battling attacks and repetitions of the same traumatic experiences time and again. I was searching for something – a lifeline, a structure, a narrative, a meaning.

I started reading business books and organisational psychology books to help me understand my life, applying business logic to the personal. That was an easy distraction. It was easy for me to be in my head, in an intellectual sense. But I still felt lost, stuck in my life and unable to find a way out. Reading was no longer enough. I was struggling to find a way to piece it all together in my mind, to align with my inner self. I could apply critical and analytical thinking to solve problems cognitively, but I was never at peace with myself or my circumstances; the stories in my mind were incoherent and incongruous.

As part of my intellectual search to provide my life with an articulation of meaning, an approach that could help me fit all the pieces of my non-linear journey together, I discovered the concept of 'design thinking'. I was approached to help design an innovation course for a business school, and as I learned more about the innovation cycle, I realised that design thinking provided a narrative for what I was already doing intuitively. It provided a framework, a logic for how I could understand my life. If it worked for products, projects and service design, why couldn't it work for me to reinvent and rebuild my own life after divorce?

In 2016, Bill Burnett and Dave Evans, professors at the Design Program at Stanford University, first proposed that design thinking can also be used to improve the lives of real human beings. In their book, *Designing Your Life: How to Build a Well-Lived, Joyful Life*, they suggest that a person can redesign their life by applying design thinking to decompartmentalised parts of their life, such as career, parenting and finances. I offer one major difference: rather than separating those elements, I've integrated them in a wholistic way.

In doing this, design thinking becomes about putting yourself at the centre of the design process, understanding your own pains, gains, needs, and desires with empathy. I had been applying design thinking at work, in my governance and volunteer roles, and even in my parenting, but I hadn't utilised it for myself.

Design thinking was an instructive framework that spoke to me and provided a narrative that I could use to help me understand the person I had become and articulate a vision for my future self. I saw it as a way to develop an alternative narrative for my life, where I was the primary beneficiary. I constructed a powerful model for myself and went through the steps of envisioning, applying theories and ideas, and iterating and testing versions of myself.

Before design thinking, whenever I wanted to improve myself, I ended up doing yet another skills-based or academic course that would help me develop my technical expertise. This was the first time I considered what I felt rather than what I knew, moving from my head to my heart, and shifting the stories that went along with that process.

Design thinking gave me the tools to identify areas in my life where I had agency in my own decision-making and journey. I went about designing my life – almost as a strategic project. There is no success or failure in design thinking, only curiosity, questioning and growth. And then you go through the whole cycle again. And again.

Writing this book very much contributed to and reflects that journey. Writing was my therapy. This book started as a diary, then became a raw and angry memoir. With time and letting go of expectations, I gained some perspective and gave it some structure before testing different versions and reaching out to others to get their perspectives. There is no final triumph in this book. But there is progress, learning and resolution. After a decade engaged in the work of designing my new self, I succeeded in releasing much of the toxicity from my life, integrating my various identities, understanding my needs at their core, and recognising my triggers and past traumas with self-compassion and humour.

Design thinking allowed me to discover and celebrate my otherness across my career, personal relationships and parenting, and ultimately emerge with a positive self-narrative. The final resolution is being at peace with myself and defining my own success and power. Being uncomfortable in my own otherness had often manifested in an anxious, curious mind. Now, 'in my own mind' is akin to Virginia Woolf's *A Room of One's Own*: a place of security, peace, liberation and creative possibility. It is also a tribute to mindfulness, a state of contentment and gratitude, vulnerability and otherness.

Rebuilding my life through design thinking

Forced to be alone without external distraction during Covid-19, I started to appreciate and listen to what was in my own mind. Certainly, the closures and lockdowns forced many of us to reframe how we give ourselves meaning. Prior to lockdowns, our life meaning was inextricably linked to the external – associated with going out and doing things with other people. We are, after all, essentially social creatures that revel in being busy and making tangible contributions to society and a difference to people. I realised during Covid that my personal meaning about *doing* should actually have first been about *being*. After reflecting on a pre-Covid relationship breakup, the thought struck me that I might have some triggers – from my family history, childhood, marriage, other relationships and experiences at work – that contributed to the circumstances I found myself in.

At its essence, design thinking deals with the individual end-user or beneficiary, that is, the person or people it is trying to serve. This isn't the forum to debate the benefits and challenges of design thinking – every framework has limitations. But it has been a useful way for me, as a divorced Jewish woman, a single mother and a professional, to provide a process and narrative to my problem – how to get my life back on track and be my true, authentic self. I took the principles of design thinking and applied them to myself.

This occurred in two parts – throughout my divorce in 2018 and over the five following years, and once again in 2023. I applied the thinking not only to disparate parts but also to my deep inner self – my perceptions, assumptions, reactions and decisions. It was only then that the transformation began.

It took me some time to understand this profound process. I was resistant to applying these ideas directly to myself. I avoided it and worked around it, living vicariously through others or through academic achievement. For a while, I did not want to dig deep. But a nagging hole remained. I didn't want to deal with myself, my traumas or my triggers. I only looked at the circumstances I found myself in, not my contribution to them or what I could change within myself to reduce their impact. Putting myself at the centre of the design thinking process allowed me to shift my inner critic, be vulnerable, and create an integrated approach to the stories I told myself about my life and my potential. This is different from a traditional application of design thinking to the compartmentalised parts of one's life. It was an emotional journey, from academic and critical to vulnerable and emotionally-integrated, from my brain to my heart.

But still, even with the first draft of this book complete, I hadn't opened fully to myself. My Jewish and Israeli identities, always part of who I am, hadn't been part of my professional or public self. They were separate. I had almost closed them off in a box, hidden among the gender-stereotypical stress and busy-ness of my day-to-day life. I hadn't thought about antisemitism, Middle Eastern politics, the first time I felt Jewish, or my emotions during my first visit to Israel for a very, very long time.

The events of 2023 cast a shadow of darkness over my world, as it did for most Jews. An unprecedented attack on young festival-goers. Heinous murders, rapes, torture and kidnappings. An increase in antisemitism and anti-Jewish activity globally. The realisation that in fact, nothing has changed for Jews and our right to live authentically and safely as Jews, particularly on campuses and in the institutions that I had served for many years – universities. There is no context that justifies the lack of safety and rights of individuals to practise culture and religion freely without fear, either in the diaspora or in their historical homeland. I felt compelled to add other lenses to my already complicated narrative.

While I can only speak from my own experience, and from a Jewish woman's perspective, I hope there is much that applies to men as well. This book is not meant to exclude men or non-Jewish people. Rather, it is about sharing a perspective to promote dialogue. I began this process years ago while waiting for my then six-year-old daughter at her Saturday morning ballet class. We were discussing which extra-curricular activities she would drop the following semester. She told me that out of all her activities, her preference was to drop school because 'writing is quite hard you know, and we have to write all day long'.

I explained that sometimes there were things we didn't have a choice about. For me, writing this book was one of those things, even though it was so very hard. It was writing that allowed me to unlock the five key stages of design thinking that we will explore in the coming chapters.

Empathise

Deeply understand yourself and your needs. Empathising involves putting yourself at the centre of decision-making. Consider yourself as the problem you are trying to solve. Now is your chance to consider all your identities with empathy. For many women, there isn't enough time in the day to check in on ourselves and ask who we are as independent beings, to slow down and listen to our inner narratives, intuition or values. Who am I when it is just me in the room? What are all my dimensions, the multiple versions of me, and how can I be authentic and vulnerable in understanding myself?

Define

Clearly outline the challenges you want to resolve by centring yourself. More often than not, women – mothers especially – put their own needs and desires last. They make decisions about themselves to fit around the rest of their lives, around chores and children, parents and pets. You have the opportunity to understand what's working, what's not, and what needs to change. You will understand your needs and make sense of the insights you have reflected on and generated. This process looks at your circumstances and what you want to change, and then asks how you might do that. It aims to get to the root of the challenge. Often, when we look at our lives, we consider problems that have a quick fix, instead of the underlying issue. This process allows us to go deeper and see more specific, innate and describable problems. Defining the problem is challenging. If we don't get the question right and establish the problem's definition and boundaries, we won't be able to produce the correct solutions. The right questions here are essential.

Ideate
Use a creative, curious, entrepreneurial and growth mindset to generate as many ideas as possible to solve the problem. Ignore the constraint of existing solutions, resources, or limits on time or money. The aim is to find as many solutions to the problem as possible, considering the different parts of your identity and their interdependencies. This is where we need to consider the 'many others' – the multitude of identities and roles that women have.

Prototype
Create some possible solutions. Once the unbounded list of ideas has been generated, determine what is feasible, particularly if time and financial resources are in short supply. Develop a realistic shortlist and plan to action your ideas. This allows you to adapt the many versions of yourself and to align them into a whole being who understands their vulnerable self.

Test and launch

Try out what you have shortlisted and see what works to meet your needs and expectations. Understand that individual approaches or solutions might fail, but you will learn from them and iterate improvements or other potential solutions. Determine which of the tested solutions should be embedded in your daily life. Commit to action so that there is a version of you that is present, whole and aligned with your values, without internal criticism or incongruity.

EMPATHISE

E mpathising is the process through which you observe your own self and interpret your life, responses and circumstances with understanding and compassion. In the empathise stage of design thinking, the interrogation of your worldview, self-perception and assumptions allows you to step into the role of empathetic observer of yourself. It offers an opportunity to capture your inner critic and explore the reasons why you behave in a certain way, without judgement.

To be empathetic, you need to understand the values that motivate you: who you are, what you stand for and what is important to you. Most of the time, when things fall apart, it is because your identity and values have been threatened. The dissidence that occurs when you are challenged to your core is a huge trigger. Understanding your intrinsic values helps you get to the core of who you are, what you stand for and the narrative you tell yourself about your place in the world. It allows you to understand yourself and your responses with self-compassion.

Discovering my inner critic

Stepping into the space of a compassionate observer of myself was not easy. For one thing, I don't have much in the way of memories. The details of my life have blurred over the years of proving and protecting myself, of looking forward, not backward. I have always avoided digging deep to remember details or linking experiences in my personal life to events in the outside world. I haven't wanted to do the hard work or go to the next level.

Whenever I tried to go to the place of the observer, I encountered a harsh voice inside my head – the inner critic. The empathetic observer was buried deep beneath, and she was hard to access. My inner critic has been active for so much of my life. It's hard to go inward when she's talking, but that's where I had to start the process, to talk to my inner critic and find out what she was trying to say. To be empathetic, I first had to examine the places where I had been cruel to and judgemental of myself. I had to drill down to find out why I had been so critical and then reframe that judgement into empathy.

I first remember negative self-talk in high school. I learned that solid work and good results weren't enough. I learned that relationships, emotional intelligence and the ability to relate to people were far more important than IQ. I was attracted to, yet repelled by academic success. I always considered it my currency and value. It defined me, but I knew it wouldn't make me happy. My mind also let me down; I couldn't control my overthinking, ruminating, planning and overworking, which wouldn't let me rest, relax or focus on my physical being. I always felt the pressure to succeed and planned for the worst-case scenario.

I took these issues into adulthood, where I was conscious of ignoring what my body told me. I avoided looking after it, eating well and sleeping enough. I breathed shallowly, making exercise difficult. I never knew I wasn't breathing right, I just assumed that was who I was. I didn't taste food; I just ate for comfort. I didn't sleep, I didn't exercise. And my body let me know. My stress bubbled into my stomach, or I would get a headache and go to bed, or I got pain in my side. But the doctors could never find anything wrong – nothing clinical, anyway.

I went to see a psychoanalyst. Psychoanalysis was a different experience from going to a psychologist, where the conversations always frustratingly focused on what I could control and rationalising others' behaviour. This, however, was about my unconscious, letting a stream of thought and words come to me, noticing where I paused, how I breathed, whether I dreamed, the non-verbal signs. It allowed me to connect again with my creative side, the sensual and the unspoken. It allowed me to think about my energy flow and what I might need to release.

I went to a health retreat. I tried tai chi, yoga, aqua aerobics, Zumba, tribal dancing, and detoxed from caffeine. I experimented with acupuncture, reflexology, massages and walks in nature. These all helped me recognise emotions I was holding – anger, resentment, loneliness, sadness. Problems with my liver; an addiction to sugar. I cried from my therapists' compassion: 'You will get back what you give.' 'You poor thing, you must be exhausted!' These acknowledgements were meaningful, but any long-term change needed to come from me. If I didn't love myself, neither would anyone else. Not the way I wanted.

I wrote in my diary:

> *I hope, I will, I expect. I'm disappointed, I'm shattered.*
> *I cringe. My mind slowly turns to a dark place. I start to*
> *tremble, my breathing hastens, and I can't listen or talk, I*
> *must breathe. I'm alone. Amongst my family. Within my*
> *marriage. My heart falls into my stomach. I feel ill. I cry, I*
> *pretend, and I keep up appearances. I shower. I cry while the*
> *hot water lashes my back. I deserve more. There is no sooth-*
> *ing for me. Only pretending I'm fine.*

I ignored what my body was telling me. Through the process of empathising, however, I finally started listening. This understanding only occurred after my divorce, after my back seized up for the umpteenth time – all the intercostal muscles were stuck, and nothing could break it. I finally went to the osteopath.

'Have you ever had glandular fever?' he asked.

'Yes, a long time ago,' I replied.

'It's still in your body. It won't show up in your blood tests, but it never leaves. It kicks you when you're down, and when you're stressed, it attacks,' he said.

That explained so much. I had a vision of the last thirty years – of the black eye bags, headaches, tiredness, fatigue, bad stomach, and sore muscles. I was relieved to find a solution, but blown away by the loss and knowledge that this hadn't needed to be my lived experience.

I knew something was missing. Despite appearances and achievements, despite the way my life looked on paper, I felt a deep hole, something preventing my full health, joy, creativity and passion for life. My inner critic was so comfortable that it invited outside critics, too. When I was younger, I put myself out there – writing articles for a local paper, running in student elections, advocating for others less fortunate. But by being in a public space, I made myself vulnerable to criticism, shame and misunderstandings. I became afraid of being in the spotlight and public criticism. I was once at a shark's den pitching for a project and felt like my values were being auctioned. No one wanted to support me. I stepped down from trying to use my voice for change. I started wondering and trying to understand what I put out into the world to elicit those responses. I didn't know I was putting something out that reflected myself back at me – my own inner critic. It was self-perpetuating, and I had to design my way out of it. I had to start with empathy for myself.

This understanding opened the door for me to embrace a new path, a new journey, a new version of me, where the past sat much more comfortably than it had before. My gut instinct had always been strong; I knew when something wasn't right. But rather than investigating and understanding my physical and emotional responses, as well as my impact on those around me, I ignored the incongruity I felt. Rather, I relied on my intellect. I'd always found it easier to study than deal with my feelings. I told myself that it didn't matter if no one liked me if I was right, intellectually and morally vindicated, and productive.

My dysfunctional heart

Lacking empathy for myself means that I haven't historically taken compliments well. Whenever someone has been kind to me, I haven't known what to do or how to respond. I so desperately wanted to be valued and acknowledged, yet I wouldn't allow myself to enjoy that attention or grow into that space. I was always waiting for the other shoe to drop. Ironically, I also always looked for acknowledgement, vindication, and an assertion of my value by 'the other'. I overcompensated by offering to help others in an effort to feel useful and appreciated. But I never actually helped myself in the same way.

My discomfort with kindness coupled with my discomfort with praise were indications that something was wrong. I had been building a brick wall around myself to avoid feeling anything.

As part of the empathising process, I began to explore how I felt grief, one of the most powerful emotions. My first experience with grief and loss was when my grandfather died. I was in Grade Five, and I didn't know he was sick. But I'll never forget my father's reaction – the hulk of a man at six feet four inches, inconsolable, returning from the funeral with his black shirt torn, the mark of a mourner in Jewish tradition.

I am stoic for those who are grieving. I organise things, I have their back, I make the eulogies, I take care of things, I don't get into my own feelings. By contrast, I can grieve in the abstract. I grieve for the world when people die in terrorist attacks. I grieved when we lost Justice Ruth Bader Ginsberg. I grieve for the pain and loss that others suffer. I grieve for the mental health issues our kids face and for all the challenges young people today must confront. I grieve for the absence of leadership among our politicians and for the future. I grieve for young women – the juxtaposition of the messages the world gives them about their own agency, voices and bodies.

I also grieve at times for my lost self. I am sad about the loss of my own opportunities – not seeing an idea to fruition, not making a project stick – or of lost friendships and relationships because I stayed true to my intrinsic values and my gut instinct. Maybe some of these expressions of grief are alternative versions of the inner critic. Yet, even within all these versions of grief, what I missed was the pure, unadulterated sadness that comes from the pain of losing myself.

To understand why that inner critic had been dominating my internal chatter and why my heart was blocked, I had to go where I didn't want to go – delving into the traumas that had defined me.

I never considered that I had been traumatised in my life. There was no terrible event, no abuse, no rape, no miscarriage, no death, no illness. Just a constant feeling of not doing enough, not being enough. I learned that trauma doesn't have to be huge, life-changing or violent to have an effect. Trauma can be lots of little put-downs, criticism, poor treatment, disrespect, loneliness and things going wrong. These moments have a cumulative effect. Microstress is caused by difficult moments that we 'register as just another bump in the road – if we register them at all. Microstresses come at us so quickly, and we're so conditioned to just working through them, that we barely recognise anything has happened'.[1]

I was always different, always associated with the 'other'. I had internalised all the contradictions of my family life. But the traumatic effects of my family's experiences were absorbed into my inner critic and, perhaps more importantly, into my decision-making across the spheres of my life. Understanding the day-to-day traumas of my life experience allowed me to understand myself much better and manage my way through letting go – not taking everything so personally, not being so defensive, and understanding the limitations and traumas of those around me.

---

[1] Cross, R., and K. Dillon. "The Hidden Toll of Microstress." *Harvard Business Review*, February 2023. Accessed May 14, 2024. https://hbr.org/2023/02/the-hidden-toll-of-microstress.

Generational trauma

The steady backdrop to my life growing up was the Holocaust, and its story – the eradication of my extended family – is etched in my soul. It seems like only yesterday that I was in primary school, sitting with my late grandfather to record the story of his early life in war-torn Europe. He told me that when he returned to his hometown after the war, his house was still standing, but it was empty. No Jews were left. This again became a reality for me when I saw the name of the town in which he was born chiselled onto the walls of the Yad Vashem Holocaust Museum in Israel, as one of many that had its Jewish population wiped out. Nothing could prepare me for the shock of that experience.

I was brought up with the Holocaust, which is not uncommon in the life of a Jew in contemporary Melbourne. I couldn't escape it; it was everywhere. Most grandparents were survivors. I remember many grandparents with camp numbers tattooed on their arms, picking up their grandchildren from school. From my diary:

> *What effect does that have on a child, knowing that you came from a survivor? That they escaped? That if it weren't for a chance, you wouldn't be here. That you need to stay standing so that the loss is explainable. Justifiable. They died so I could survive. The enormity. A wall. Migration. Refugees. Social justice. These have permeated every aspect of my being. It's who I am, it's what I'm a product of.*
>
> *Auschwitz, a poor, rural village outside Krakow in Poland, is broken into the labour camp, and Birkenau, the death camp. In the Hungarian memorial room at Auschwitz, etched in black stone, I saw my name. The name of my grandfather's aunt, who died in Auschwitz, is the same as mine. It embodies me. I can't escape it. It confronted me with my collective past. The lack of family history, of knowledge,*

of photos. We have no evidence of our existence. Part of the black hole in my heart is the black hole in my family history. It is incomplete. And it makes me feel different. A square peg in a round hole.

Early memories feature pictures of subjects of Mengele's experiments: emaciated, starved figures, walking skeletons. Dehumanised. I studied the Holocaust – at school, at university. In every city and town I ever visited, I have followed the trail of Jewish destruction across the globe.

This trauma has defined so much of who I am: the sense of otherness, the immigrant experience, my strong social justice and human rights values, my career and volunteer choices, my roles in community and philanthropy. The Holocaust has affected me and my relationships in so many ways. My choice to marry a Jewish man, my grandfather's fear of dogs, my grandmother's hoarding, the loss and grief of what never was, and the guilt for being here.

The narrative of Jewish oppression, suffering and self-reliance infused me from a young age. It affected my psyche. It simultaneously gave me a sense of connection and belonging paired with a feeling of otherness and difference. It is the foundation of my identity: my sense of self and my otherness.

I don't remember the first time I ever felt Jewish in an existentialist sense. I just was. I suppose it was at university – I had never met a non-Jewish person my own age until then. And I felt like I had an obligation to teach them, to show them who we were – as a culture, a religion, a people, a race, a nation and all the ways Jews have been defined throughout history (always as the other). It is complex and difficult to understand. It has only been recently that I really came to understand it myself. When I was younger, the primary way I defined myself as a Jew was through the experience of the Holocaust.

I immersed myself in stories about Jewish responses to the Holocaust. I have read the biographies and autobiographies of survivors – stories that left me with many questions about life, human nature, and my own place in the world. The mass genocide is unfathomable. Nothing was left. It was as though they never existed. How could there be no Jews left in the thriving communities from which my grandparents came? How does a person create a life for themselves knowing that this is what humanity is capable of? And I still ask myself those questions today.

In my family, many of the manifestations of this generational trauma were in relation to food. When my brother and I were little, we spent a lot of time with my paternal grandparents. I remember our Shabbat dinners – chicken soup, gefilte fish and schnitzel, which were my grandmother's specialties, and matzo balls at Pesach. My grandmother told me all about the fish that her mother sold in her shop in Poland, and she was always the go-to for repairing our clothes, as her father did in his tailor shop. She taught us about immigration, the migrant experience, Israel, and the sacrifices one makes for family. Her food was the backdrop for sharing her life drama.

Still, she never really assimilated and was always critical of life in Australia. Actually, she was critical of life everywhere and was entirely politically incorrect. She never learned English or how to drive. She was physically in Australia, but parts of her were being lived elsewhere; in her haunted past, on another continent, in a different world far away. Her disjointedness and buried pains stayed with me. So did the comfort eating.

The pages of my life are stained with the echoes of what has come before me, and I'm sure it will leave its print on the pages to come.

These histories have given me and my children a fundamental sense of who we are, where we come from and how we got here. They've given us a love of history, curiosity, wonder and travel. Yet along with that is a great unspoken loss – a pressure to achieve and make up for lost opportunities and unfulfilled potential. It is a negative approach to identity, and one that affected me greatly.

As the Holocaust was the background to crafting my early identity and life story, my life in Australia was also fraught with conflict. I am a product of two different cultures, and I come from both sides of the tracks. One set of grandparents was well-off, established businesspeople. The others were factory workers who couldn't speak English and never assimilated. I was everything to all of them, and they lived vicariously through me, manifesting high expectations and a pressure to perform. I was the other wherever I turned.

How the past sits in me

I don't know if anyone really remembers their early years or if we are simply reminded by family stories and photos. As I began to peel back the layers of my life, I discovered many pieces of the past coming forward.

One of my first discoveries was the imperative I felt to serve others at my own expense. The notion of self-sacrifice was ingrained in me throughout my childhood. 'Others before you sacrificed so you could be here. Don't let their sacrifice go to waste.' I spent hours and hours in volunteer and community work, which was an escape but also reflective of my need for approval and recognition. I was hypersensitive to criticism and rejection.

These dynamics also had a positive aspect. They drove me to achieve. I was the first in many ways: the first grandchild, the first to finish school, the first to go to university, the first with any degree, the first cousin, the first to get married, the first to get divorced, the first feminist, the first swing voter. This push and pressure still sits in me. The 'firsts' that made me stand out were a blessing and a curse. I absorbed all the energies and emotions around me. Whatever someone else was carrying, I felt.

I beat myself up over every wrong word and bad reaction. I wore my emotions on my sleeve, and it was clear to the world when I was unhappy. I didn't sleep. I couldn't get out of my head. I found it hard to let anything go. My perfectionism and disappointment in myself – my inner critic – and the constant, gnawing feeling of not fulfilling my potential through circumstance or choice followed me everywhere. This emotional inhibition and unrelenting standards meant there was little joy or pleasure in my life.

Family stories are crucial to understanding your identity. Knowing where you come from, where you fit into a broader familial and social or cultural context, the stories of your ancestors, how you are similar and different from your forebears, and what you learn from their experiences all help you define your own narrative. Vestiges of the past were in me, but at the same time, I was forming something else: an independent version of myself, one that was self-compassionate and able to move on from past experiences. But that side was lonely. It was battling against generations of embedded patterns.

Coming out the other end

Through this lonely process of understanding myself through my family history, I learned to take a compliment and not be suspicious when someone is kind. Although I am still often guarded, waiting for the rug to be pulled out from under me, I recognise the critical voice inside of me, and let it go.

Once I learned to be kinder to myself, I was kinder to others. I became more patient, less demanding, and less inclined to take things personally. I also discovered the power of my resilience. I can solve a problem, sit in the pain and recover through the adversity. I can walk away from people when they are toxic for me, when there is incongruence with my ethics and values, when I can't be associated with something anymore, or when I feel unvalued.

Empathy first

The first and most crucial part of the design process is putting yourself in the shoes of the person you are trying to serve – that is, *you*. Understand who you are and what you see, hear, feel and think across the domains of your life.

To begin this process, ask:

- What are my values?
- How do I understand and work towards meaning in my life?
- Do I have a sexual, religious or cultural identity or affinity?
- How does being a woman of a certain age affect my self-perception and how I see myself in the world?
- What are my needs and desires? Why are they important to me?
- What is my vision for myself? What does success look like for me across all the spheres of my life?
- What is going well? What is keeping me awake at night?
- What is my inner critic saying? What does she tell me?
- How does she manifest? Where did she come from?

- What relationships are not working for me? Why aren't they working?
- What kind of relationships would I like to have?
- How am I kind to myself?
- How do I show resilience?
- What self-perceptions are caused by trauma?
- What can I change or release? How do I do this?

DEFINE

When we look at the define element of design thinking, we are really seeking to identify the problem and set the parameters of the challenge. Defining usually starts with a 'how might we' sentence, considering different points of view in an empathetic way. In this case, I am, the beneficiary. There are many intersections with my identity and many ways I could define the problems. So I asked myself – how do I reconcile the many versions of 'otherness'?

The many 'others'

Once I was open to seeing myself with empathy and compassion, I saw many identities that were all 'others'. Each defined me in different ways and contributed to the person others see. I am a mother, daughter, sister, ex-wife, colleague, friend, partner, lover, philanthropist, board member, and more. I have been a lawyer, academic, strategist, governance expert, manager and specialist in gender, refugees and disability. I have run writing retreats, started a blog, founded a women's empowerment program and sat on various boards. Meanwhile, the thing I was the least expert in was myself. How could I find the time to understand myself? I had full responsibility for the house, the kids, and an emotional and social load. I was tired and busy.

Upon reflection, I discovered that many of my activities were distractions. Certainly, they served a purpose and were attempts at giving myself meaning and value. Often, they nourished me. For a long time, they were almost exclusively in the Jewish community, trying to fill the need for a Jewish home. But they also exhausted and drained me. Ultimately, they didn't give me what I needed. They kept me busy, distracted me and had positive impacts on others, but at the end of the day, I was still left with me.

That said, I also discovered that I am more complex and contradictory than I once thought. I have multiple identities, and different ones come to the fore at different times. The essence of being reveals a beautiful truth about who I am, who we all are – I am not alone in this. The multifaceted identities of women are complex. Recognising my contrasting needs and desires, the multitude of considerations, and the push-pull factors that influence my decisions has been a work in progress. This process is made more difficult for all women because it is not supported by our legal, economic, cultural or structural systems. For me, understanding and integrating the multifaceted nature of my identity was key to defining myself. Otherness was a key part of the defining process.

Jewish

Jewish identity is complex. It is a combination of negative and positive elements – persecution and pride. It was always an essential part of my cultural and traditional self and I valued keeping the stories of my family and the immigrant experience alive. I went to a Jewish day school and when I got to university, I didn't know how to manage my Jewish identity in the broader world. I didn't know how to explain why my parents wouldn't let me date a non-Jew. I didn't know how to explain why I ate dinner with my family every Friday night or why antisemitism was different from other forms of racism. I didn't have the words to explain why I required more than policies about equality, inclusion, respect and safety.

It wasn't until recently, as I re-educated myself about the history of antisemitism, understanding the progressive left and far right, and the fragility of Jewish society, that I finally found the words. We are a vulnerable people. I understand it may not seem that way. We focus on education, tolerance and relationships to build ourselves up in the diaspora and become part of the fabric of a socially cohesive society. We don't generally look any different. We are seen as privileged. But we are vulnerable. Our inclusion is not set in stone. It can be taken away. It isn't enshrined anywhere other than in Israel.

Israeli

I was eighteen the first time I visited Israel. It wasn't just a reunion with family that I had never met before, it was a lesson in how Israel's military struggles affect each family. My uncle was the only surviving paratrooper in his unit during the Suez Canal Crisis; people thought he would never walk again after a bullet lodged in his back. The injury prompted my grandparents, who had already immigrated once, to immigrate to Australia, so their other children wouldn't be at risk: more sacrifice.

I studied Middle Eastern politics at university and completed an exchange program in Israel. I always considered myself Israeli first, Australian second. I was homesick for Israel when I wasn't there. I spent my time learning about and understanding issues relating to the Law of Return, the events of 1948 and how the international community perceived Israel.

When I returned to Israel after twenty odd years with my children, I cried. I cried at every historical site. I cried every time I heard the national anthem. I cried at the Wailing Wall, although I am not religious at all. I cried when I saw a young army officer with a gun strapped to their back. I cried for their reality. The pain and pride it evokes is indescribable. It encapsulates me. On her first trip there, my daughter said, 'Now I understand you much better, Mummy.' And I cried.

Israel's international standing at the UN has always been fascinating for me. Israel stands simultaneously as both an outsider and a reflection of the democratic ideal. In 1998 I wrote an article as a final year intern about Israel's attempt to obtain permanent membership in one of the five regional blocks that would allow it decision-making powers: the African Group, Asia and the Pacific Group, Eastern European Group, the Latin American and Caribbean Group, the Western European and Other Group. To be accepted into a group, Israel needed consensus from the other members. Without membership of a regional block, Israel was excluded from being elected to leadership positions on most bodies in the UN system. It was only in 2014 that Israel was granted its sovereign equality at the UN, a principle enshrined in the UN Charter in 1945 – a right already in existence when Israel was established.

In 2016 I attended the Commission on the Status of Women Meeting at the UN in New York. It was a bucket list event for me, a foray into the world of international diplomacy and a place where I thought impactful decisions would be made for good. However, as the event continued and draft resolutions were being circulated and shared, I realised one reality: Israel was dispensable in those deliberations and negotiations. In a system of block voting and give and take, countries were willing to condemn or ignore Israel to progress their own agenda.

And nothing has changed. What I had written all those years ago as a Jewish woman all came back to me. The horrors of sexualised violence and terror and the blatant hypocrisy of UN Women and the international community slapped me starkly. Again. They weren't holding themselves to their own standards. They were ignoring evidence, failing to fulfil their own purpose, and denying the experiences and traumas of Israeli and Jewish women. My women. Our women.

It forced me, grieving for these tragedies that kept unfolding, to reconsider my identity – as a woman, as a Jew, as an Israeli. It rocked me, as it did many others, to my core. I had the realisation that we are on our own – we are the ultimate other.

Divorce

My marriage, and therefore my life and career, were defined by my caring responsibilities. I allowed it to happen. Part of it was a cultural expectation – the stereotypical 'Jewish mother'. I didn't maintain my own identity. As I went from my parents' home to my matrimonial home, I didn't know how. I didn't know what it meant to be me, to live by or with myself. I was just twenty-three years old when I got married, three weeks after finishing law school. I hadn't even started my first job, but I already had a husband and a mortgage. I realise now that I got married to escape from the pressure to be something, to do something. I didn't know that I was the only one who could help me escape. At the end of the day, I was trying to escape from myself.

I had expectations of an equal share – splitting housework, chores, cooking and contribution – but that didn't happen. I earned less. I did more around the house. I did the cooking and shopping. I made the social arrangements. I didn't engage with the finances.

Mine was a textbook case of all the gender-stereotypical things that happen in a relationship, and the resentment grew. Women undertake household chores at considerably higher rates than men. Women bear the brunt of doing the housework, emotionally supporting the children, project managing the schedule and, for those who are so inclined, trying to develop their own careers. It comes at a cost, one that is not valued and certainly not translated into any form of tangible pay. Yes, I did it because I wanted to, because I thought it was the right thing to do at the time, and because I wanted to be there for my children. I was complicit in my own circumstances, failing to understand the mental, emotional, physical and financial toll it would take. And I kept nothing separate for myself – except a remnant of who I once was.

I once calculated that the value of my contribution, based on the equivalent number of hours I spent managing the household, would equate to $100,000 a year. And I performed this labour on top of working full time, managing a team, voluntary and governance roles, writing, other social enterprise projects, continued learning, and my own emotional stress and mental exhaustion.

I have always been told that I embodied resilience and strength, and that I would land on my feet because I was smart, capable and tough. I found this unhelpful, and sometimes even tormenting. How could I be fine if I had totally lost myself and was stretched by everything that I was trying to juggle? Therapists, family and friends told me I should change my expectations of those around me. Perhaps that was true, but without the space to care for myself, how could I care for others? I felt alone. Different. Other. I asked the psychologist I was seeing at the time, 'At what point do I stop fighting for myself if this is the rest of my life?'

The same is true of the isolation of divorce. Women often walk away from what they are entitled to, because they are too tired, too stressed, too poor, or too busy with the kids or trying to make ends meet to fight for themselves. The Jewish tradition has an additional divorce requirement – a religious divorce alongside the civil one, where the husband releases the wife as his property and she is told not to have sexual relations with any other man for three months, to ensure paternity if she is pregnant at the time of divorce. Both systems make the women feel like the other.

M(otherhood)

I found motherhood exhausting and lonely, even when I was surrounded by lots of other mothers. I also found that motherhood can be competitive. It cost me friends, especially those who lacked the empathy to understand particular challenges when it comes to children who might not fit the neurotypical mould, or parenting styles that don't include distraction with technology or treating your children like a trophy or a friend.

It's hard to dig deep to understand a child's thinking and strengths. It's difficult to find a way to relate, to find a bond or commonality when so much of what I saw was both the best and the worst of me encapsulated in another human. I wanted to let them know they were loved, even when I was angry, upset or disappointed.

My eldest son had hearing and auditory process challenges that manifested in less-than-desirable behaviours and interactions. It required project management in gross and fine motor skills, social skills, speech therapy, paediatricians, test after test, session after session, allergies, asthma, clinics, hearing aids, social exclusion, mental health challenges, my own lost friendships, changing schools. Starting again.

How do we, as mothers, maintain ourselves and give our loved ones what they need? How do we bring them into our circle of self and still preserve ourself? Caring for people – children, friends, partners, parents – with their own emotional, mental, physical and behavioural challenges can turn you into a shadow of who you thought you were. You don't know what you are going to get or what you will deal with in motherhood, or how to push yourself to stay positive, project manage, advocate, organise, and see your children through their challenges.

There is little in the way of information or stories about how those who care for or support loved ones don't lose themselves in that process of caring. We need more stories from women who have supported loved ones, grieved for a future that wasn't going to happen, and dealt with the pain and feeling of selfishness or failure when they let go, say 'I can't do it any more', and ask for help.

I worried. All the time. I worried about the logistics of doing the right thing for each of the kids. I worried when I relied on a friend to pick them up and drop them at home for me. I worried about not spending enough time with each of them separately or together as a family. I worried that I worried too much. I worried that all this worry meant I was missing out on really enjoying time with my children. I worried that if I didn't worry and think about things, then something would go wrong. I worried that I was worrying their childhoods away. I worried for all of our futures. And I worried alone. For me, there was no bigger trigger for anxiety than motherhood. Perhaps another Jewish stereotype.

Motherhood changed my life, my priorities and my interests. It stretched and pushed me. It challenged my assumptions, a process of change that began with a shift in what I considered to be a productive use of time.

Much has been written about what it means to be a good mother and a bad mother. Authors like Ayelet Waldman in *Bad Mother* and Wednesday Martin in *Primates of Park Avenue* write about the stress of motherhood and mothers who try to be everything to everyone, then lose themselves or become ill in the process. Others, like Ann-Marie Slaughter in *Unfinished Business*, Sheryl Sandberg in *Lean In*, and Arianna Huffington in *Thrive*, write about having it all and the need to value the care economy. But the bottom line is that the structural and cultural inhibitors to women being able to be financially independent with young children – the wage gap, the superannuation gap, the tax system and the cost of childcare – mean that sometimes it is just not worth the effort. And then motherhood becomes another other; another isolating point of difference between you and the rest of the world.

Financial

A woman's view on financial management goes to the heart of her relationships with her parents, partners, inheritances and values. When the question, 'Would you be able to take care of your affairs if something happened to your partner or parent?' was asked to a group of professional women, the response was fascinating. While some vehemently insisted that women should maintain their own funds for a rainy day, others felt that it was an antithesis to their marriage to insist on independent finances. I believe that economic empowerment and financial literacy are key to independence and gender equity. While women invest in their families and communities, men tend to invest in themselves. In failing to invest in themselves, many women perpetuate the financial challenges that are holding them back. From my diary:

> I realised with a panic that I had never had my own money and that I was largely financially dependent and certainly financially illiterate. Somehow, I fell into the gender-stereo-typical role of not dealing with the household budget and finances. From the time I finished my undergraduate degree at university, any money I earned went into a pooled fund. I never had my own bank account. Not having my own money meant that I was not financially independent. Not having recompense for the work I did made me feel undervalued. I did not have a buffer for a rainy day. That made me feel very insecure.

The absence of my own income also limited my ability to progress in my career. It restricted my ability to pay for professional development, become a member of professional organisations and go to conferences. Since my divorce, I have worked full time, continued my education and bought a house. I have somehow managed to earn what I needed to give the kids what they needed. Sometimes I've had less than $10,000 in the bank and didn't know how I would pay the next mortgage instalment. When I applied for mortgage relief, the bank told me that they couldn't provide it because they didn't think I would be able to repay them and kept my rate at the highest variable. Yet I managed to pay the mortgage, despite my alienation and lack of support from a financial system that refused to recognise the plight of single mothers.

Professional

As I was growing up, every now and then I went to my grandparents'
office and 'worked'. I made photocopies and answered the phones;
as I got older, I became more involved in other office tasks. My
maternal grandparents built a successful tyre and mechanic fran-
chise, and as I grew up, I knew that my grandfather was revered as
a business owner. He was the boss with a calculator that spat out
paper, a lovely pen set and his own separate office. I wanted to be
just like that.

My search for professional meaning has morphed as my career
has progressed from lawyer to academic, to projects, strategy, governance and impact. I've moved from technical specialist to manager
to director. When I was younger, I fell into the trap of expectations.
I had the grades and the highest entry score, which was required
for law. Law was the hardest course to get into and, in my mind,
therefore the best.

I never actually wanted to be a lawyer. I almost failed the first
year. I was used to being at the top of the class, and all of a sudden,
I was among intellectual equals. I was just like everybody else. All I
knew, because I had been told over and over again, was that I could
do anything. Of course, I know now that is not true at all. It only
sets people – women especially – up for failure.

I undertook my first internship straight out of law school, in what
was also the first year of my marriage. I quickly found that formal
education and great marks are no match for practical experience or
emotional intelligence. I learned a lot about the world that year: the
value of money, the cost of living, and how to receive instructions and
ask for help. I also came face-to-face with the gendered nature of the
law. Thirty years ago, I was paid $14,000 less than my male counterparts

for the same level job. I won the Ally McBeal Award (named for the '90s legal show), which made fun of the length of my skirts. It was humiliating. I felt like a second-class citizen through all of this, and I left the legal profession upon becoming qualified. The Other.

It was during this time that I first experienced sexism, came face-to-face with the stale-pale-male, and found myself reduced to a 'less than' for my gender. It was also the first time I realised there was a glass ceiling that I didn't want to pander to. In order to have the home life I wanted, I realised I would need to compromise. I bowed out, thinking that academia would be a better match for my personality and lifestyle. This, in turn, facilitated the gender stereotypes that were beginning to form and perpetuate in my marriage. My first professional decision was based on my gender, when I assumed academia would be more flexible, inclusive and accessible.

I received a scholarship to undertake a Masters/PhD. I lectured, tutored, and became increasingly involved with refugee advocacy and governance roles in community organisations. Through this, I gained exposure to the media, organised events and conferences, budgeted strategic planning, managed working committees and gained skills in community development and advocacy. I led without authority.

I also became a content expert on Australia's refugee policy. My PhD thesis was in the same area, so my technical and adaptive skills developed through this time. But the dichotomy between my position as chair or committee member and as tutor or junior lecturer was tangible. A schism emerged, a lack of balance and equilibrium between my paid and volunteer roles. Even at this early stage, there were multiple professional identities that were misaligned between the work I did in community and the work I did as a professional. It was almost as though I was managing two different pathways at the same time, and I was never fully able to commit to either. I didn't always feel that I could bring my whole self to work, and worried that I needed to diminish parts of myself to progress. The internal schisms remained and left me feeling different, incomplete and other.

Midway through my PhD, I moved to London and undertook some teaching and research roles. One project sticks out in my mind. My boss insisted that, as the more senior person, he felt entitled to go first in the byline. I had done the work, yet I was sidelined in the contribution acknowledgement. I thought this was how the world worked and felt that I didn't have a choice but to give in. However, my resentment about the gendered dynamic in the workplace and the feeling of being invisible and undervalued began to grow.

I presented at international conferences. I was published. I was on track for a stellar academic career. When an opportunity to lecture in the law school came up, I took it and worked two jobs. I worked on research during the day and prepared lectures at night. I managed because I was alone most of the time. I had some friends, but I often ate dinner alone and filled my time with extra work. I was motivated and wanted to progress in my career. I didn't realise I was permitting a dynamic that would lead down an inevitable path in my personal life. The choice of partner is one of the most crucial decisions we can make. I was twenty-three. I didn't know any better.

Completing my PhD was one of the defining moments in my life. In many ways, it was my escape from being at home with young children, as something that could be managed around their needs. I went to coffee shops and drafted and redrafted. I took drafts with me to the hospital when my son had his grommets inserted, tonsils removed and adenoids taken out. I worked during the kids' daytime naps and at night when I was on my own. It kept me sane. The department went through cuts and changes, and I had a couple of supervisors over that period. I also had my second child. After I submitted to my examiners – one an established senior male academic and the other an up-and-coming female academic – I could relax and take stock.

I waited a long nine months for my results. I couldn't understand what was taking so long. While I was waiting, I applied for a number of research jobs at the university. In one of the first interviews, I was asked why there was a gap on my CV for the year I was at home with my kids. I replied that I had two small children, not realising the implications of that statement. Apparently, I came in second and was told by the main interviewer that I reminded him of his daughter, but I just wasn't the right fit. I wish I knew then what I know now about the way the world works.

For my PhD, I received one pass with no alterations from the more senior assessor. This was highly unusual and a great compliment to the original contribution of the work to the field. The other assessment alleged the complete opposite; the work had no value whatsoever, and my PhD should be failed immediately, with no opportunity to rewrite. I had to sit before two panels and make a case for my defence. Ultimately, I made it through, but it put me off academia forever.

Most PhD candidates go through some trauma or defining rite of passage. I often wonder if my PhD was worthwhile, but acknowledge that in some ways it was my saviour and escape during that period of my life. It offered a little piece just for me in a world I couldn't control and struggled to cope in.

The PhD took about two years longer than I wanted and left me in limbo during that time, unsure of my career prospects, putting my life on hold to wait for the outcome. It took six years out of my career. I was on scholarship, which meant I wasn't earning any substantive income and was socially isolated because I was working on my own. I couldn't go to conferences or network. However, it also allowed me to develop deep expertise, was manageable with small kids at home, and set me on a career trajectory where I was able to position myself as an intermediary between corporate and academic partners to facilitate progress. In some ways, it saved my life. In others, it crushed me. Either way, I experienced it alone, as an other.

Entrepreneurial

A pivotal moment occurred after I completed my PhD and decided I didn't want to pursue an academic career, when I approached a not-for-profit organisation to undertake a project. I told the chair I would be happy to do it voluntarily. He told me not to be ridiculous and asked me to come up with an hourly rate. I had no idea where to place myself in the market, so I reverted to an academic pay scale, which is where I had spent almost all of my career. When I came back to him, he doubled it. He also suggested that I get an ABN and set myself up as a consultant. I had never thought I would be able to work for myself. It made a huge difference to have someone encourage me to test a path I had never pictured myself travelling. This was my first lesson in how difficult but important it is to value your services, especially when your service is your brain.

As a result, I started my own consulting business and learned about the world of philanthropy and social impact. When I told my kids that I'd be working three days a week from an office and two days a week from home, their reactions were gorgeous. My eight-year-old son was so proud of me. He'd been asking for months when I was going back to work and was so excited when I told him. He even told me that I looked amazing the first day I got dressed up to go to work. My daughter was hysterical. 'We'll be rich!' she shouted with glee. 'Not quite,' I said. Every day, when I picked my son up from school, he asked me how my day at work had been. He wanted to know everything – what I was doing and what I was writing.

Starting my own consulting and research business in my late thirties was exhausting and intense, but it made me happier than I had felt in such a long time. Why? Because I had something for myself. Because I could bring all the parts of me together. This was never in my plan. I never thought I would be a consultant owning my own company. Once the business was established, I didn't know whether I would get any contracts, and then I got two at the same time, and I negotiated my own terms so that I could work school hours and be there for my kids. My consultancy has allowed me to show a risk appetite and an entrepreneurial spirit. It has shown me one of the benefits of otherness.

Understanding my story of otherness

For so many years, parts of myself were disconnected. In my day-to-day activities, I struggled with which persona to prioritise. If I went to the gym, it took time away from my work. If I wrote, I couldn't go to the gym. If I saw a therapist, it took time away from something else. I was decompartmentalised. Yet these elements were so interdependent – what happened at home affected and drove my decisions in my career. My childhood and relationships with my parents and grandparents affected my marriage and parenting choices. Incongruity remained, mostly in my stomach and head. I didn't have an integrated, holistic definition or narrative of myself – I hadn't self-actualised. I didn't understand that I was greater than the sum of my parts and required my own story.

One of the ways I tried to integrate these ideations was by designing and facilitating a women's empowerment initiative called Project Deborah. This place-based program aimed to empower and develop capabilities in Jewish professional women across several spheres – leadership, branding, community, relationships, finance and governance – so they could thrive and fulfil their own ambitions. It offered exactly what I needed in my own life. The response to the calls for expressions of interest was staggering and indicated a real need for such programs and interventions for women in their communities.

Project Deborah was named after the judge, prophetess, military leader, and the only woman in the Old Testament to stand on her own merit and not be identified or defined by her husband. Deborah is also my Hebrew name, and the name of a great-great-aunt who died in Auschwitz. All the parts of me came together in this program and its name. In Judaism, names tell your story and give you meaning. Project Deborah gave my life meaning, purpose and lessons that I would take with me on my journey to understand myself and my otherness. Over time I began to envision and describe myself not in relation to specific work, circumstances or people. Instead I learned to integrate all those different identities into one narrative and measure meaning and success differently.

Defining otherness

The second stage of the design thinking process is the attempt to define the problem you want to solve. In my case, how I might integrate all my identities, my otherness, into one narrative. To begin this process, ask:

- How do I put myself out into the world?
- How does the world perceive me?
- What are the different versions of me that I want to focus on?
- Where and when have I felt my most authentic self?
- When have I felt alone or different?

IDEATE

In the preceding stage, I began to define and clarify my identity through a series of questions, enquiries and examinations. The ideate phase of design thinking considers a multiplicity of solutions from different perspectives and identities to ask, what is possible?

First, I had to deconstruct myself. Then, I needed to put myself back together with a way forward for each of those deconstructed yet interdependent elements. My design thinking journey continued into the 'ideate' phase, exploring my own self-definitions through writing and narrative.

I went through a process of self-observation – understanding where my energy flowed from, what activities I was drawn to, and what I wanted to learn. I also investigated sources of shame, regret, pride and control, and the assumptions I made about how I do things and what was expected of me.

What would I do in my career, across my relationships, my physicality and my creativity, if time and money were not considerations?

What would I want my life to be like? What would I release? How would I spend my time? What kind of leader would I want to be? For myself? For others?

Over this period of ideation, I reflected on my own sense of difference and otherness without searching for the validation of being right, expert, smart or strong.

I discovered that my need to be right and my ambition were trying to plug holes in myself, to do more, be more, achieve more, be valued more. And I *have* achieved a lot. I have a PhD, EMBA, a successful career, have made contributions to the community and positively affected the trajectories of many women. Why wasn't it enough? I have learned that I should set my own values-based parameters of success. When those values and my activities are incongruent, then I can walk away. I don't need to stay. It isn't failure; the focus should be on learning, growing, and trying to understand what works for me. It is my own, rather than society's, measures that count. In a world of otherness, I learned, independence is critical.

Independence

Before I began the design process, I thought of myself as dependent in a system that didn't allow me to thrive. Many parts of me had shut down and were no longer within reach. I had to find them again.

I started to understand myself better. As I exercised more, I learned that I wasn't breathing properly; my intercostal muscles were locked, which meant that I ran out of breath quickly. I learned that I had a problem with the veins in my legs, a problem that had always been there and slowed me down. I started dealing with my health issues.

I went to galleries and opened the creative part of my mind again. I earned enough money to support myself and the kids – financial independence. I bought a house and a car. I took the kids on holidays. I did things for myself that I never thought I would – from mundane activities like mowing the lawn and taking out the rubbish to bigger actions like dealing with my health and undertaking therapy for intergenerational trauma. I made decisions for myself. It was liberating. It hasn't been easy or linear. I started thinking about a life where I understood my own emotions, how my interactions affected others, what I wanted for myself and what I wanted to put out into the world. I better understood my own body and I became more aware of my own triggers around my values. I recognised how I wanted to be communicated with and appreciated.

One of the self-revelations that most shocked me through this ideation process related to my own feminist ideology. I always thought I was a staunch feminist, with an explanation for everything through a feminist and gender lens and an understanding of the cultural, social, policy and systemic barriers that women face. But as I looked inward and discovered my new self, I realised I had internal responses that countered my own idea of feminism. I desired a reciprocal relationship with a loving partner that made me feel safe and secure. I realised that financial independence didn't mean I shouldn't accept the offer from others to pay for dinner. I learned that keeping my eye on the north star – my vision for my life – was more important than winning every little argument. I understood that both men and women needed trust and psychological safety, and that men also suffered from their own issues – golden handcuffs and toxic masculinity. The new version of myself saw men as partners rather than the cause of the world's problems, and recognised that there were enough kind men out there who also wanted to effect change.

I reflected over my life to remember when I felt the most Jewish, the most feminine, the most Israeli, the most different. I delved deep to see where I experienced moments of joy and contentment. I reminded myself of the activities I loved as a child. I remembered the moments of awe and calm, freedom and independence, and where they'd come from. And it surprised me.

For years, I had closed myself off to the arts. Now I started taking myself to galleries and tested my memory about the artists I used to love and study at school. I would sit and stare with wonder at the walls and roofs of galleries for hours, considering my emotions as I observed what was in front of me but also what was going on inside me – how art related to the stories of my own life. A reconnection. Music, art and literature all came back to me. They re-entered my mind and connected with my heart and my whole being.

One of my favourite objects in my home is a Chagall lithograph. Chagall is my favourite artist; he represents the history of the Jewish people. The roof of the Paris Opera House, which he painted in contrast to the gothic style of the rest of the building, symbolises success in the non-Jewish world. It highlights the contrast between antiquity and whimsy, dark and light, and celebrates culture, the arts, beauty and awe.

Another favourite item is my bookshelf with a ladder; my aspiration is to have floor-to-ceiling bookshelves stacked with books and be surrounded by stories. Stories are my connection to myself and the world, my saviour and escape. They speak to me and for me. I bought these items during my marriage, and they were the two pieces I took when I left the matrimonial home. They symbolised me as an independent self. Woman. Divorced. Jewish. Other.

Impact

Part of the ideating process involves understanding how you impact those around you. It is about your relationships and how you create meaning with others. In trying to find connection and meaning with those around me, I needed to develop a self-narrative that is inter-dependent and relational, part of a bigger picture. Often, however, my intentions are not congruent with my behaviours or impact.

We looked at this during Project Deborah, designing T-shirts on which we listed our values and what we wanted to put out into the world on the front, with our behaviours on the back. I care for my family, but I resent the fact that I don't have time for me; health is a core value, but I often ignore exhaustion, injury and pain. I want to do the best job I can at work but avoid taking unpopular actions that might be right for the business because I want to be liked.

I learned the impact of this schism the hard way. I learned that you need to share your story, goals and ambitions. But you also need to meet people where they are and bring them on your journey. One of the things I most regret about Project Deborah is having focused only on the participants, rather than looking outside the group to develop a pathway that I could share with community organisations who would welcome them with their ideas, innovations and energy.

Project Deborah was the ultimate lesson in relational impact. The wider community wasn't ready for these women. I was too focused on bringing along the individuals who were participating, and didn't seek buy-in for the program and my vision to scale up and replicate to other areas or underserved populations. It was the impetus for much growth and reflection. I have asked myself many times how I might do it differently next time.

There is still a need for place-based programs like Project Deborah.

A decade later the problems haven't changed. The gender pay gap, women's safety, systemic changes, family violence, the lack of women in leadership, women's untapped economic resource, the need for shared care, better childcare support and leave arrangements, the discrepancy in superannuation, unconscious bias, the need for mentoring, and many more issues are still pressing.

Project Deborah was one of the highlights of my career. However, I believe these empowerment, leadership and professional development courses can only take us so far. Without doing the hard work on ourselves, understanding our inner critic, having empathy for ourselves, and bringing our whole selves, we won't be able to move forward in a tangibly different way.

Part of my ideation process also involved mentoring others. This has given me much joy and meaning. I mentored a young lawyer looking to establish mental health support for her peers. I mentored an unemployed person to find their first job in decades. I mentored a young Indigenous woman in a start-up. I have mentored formally and informally with the aim of having a positive impact, meeting others where they are at, and positively influencing futures – theirs as well as mine.

Ideation

Through the ideation phase, I tested different ways of answering the questions about how I integrated the different parts of myself and absorbed my otherness to become an independent woman. To narrate and measure my life by my own standards and in relation to the impact I have on others.

In this ideation phase, we ask what all the possibilities are to help us answer our defined problem.

To begin this process, ask:

- What would I do in my career, across my relationships, my physicality and my creative being if time and money were not considerations?
- Am I financially literate and able to access and manage my own finances?
- How do I engage with the arts?
- What are my favourite objects? How do they make me feel? Why?
- What kinds of work, activities and causes give me energy?
- What am I most proud of?
- What do I regret or feel shame for?
- What assumptions about myself as an independent woman are real? What needs to be reassessed?
- What do I want to learn? How do I want to grow?

PROTOTYPE

Prototyping refers to putting together a basic working model. After understanding myself with empathy, asking what I want to change, considering the different versions of myself, and generating different visions for my future, it is time to try integrating it all into a working model.

I started looking at how far I had come, understanding my triggers, working to detangle my past and dealing with things I had avoided for a long time. I acknowledged and sat in my otherness.

But I found each of these versions, even as they came together in an independent me, to be relatively compartmentalised. Something was still missing. I had come a long way through this whole process in understanding the essence of an independent me, but I also needed to stop thinking about it in such an academic way.

In this process, I challenged my assumptions and revealed my contradictions across all spheres of my life. And I wrote, whenever I could and about whatever was on my mind, to reconcile those differences through being vulnerable, as a divorced woman and a Jew.

Vulnerability

For a long time, my 'minimum viable product' (to use business-speak) was my intellect and technical expertise. I lived vicariously through my contributions to work and governance roles. They were an escape and gave me meaning. Yet when I reflected on my career, I saw a series of missed opportunities and missed connections. I was scared to put myself out there. I feared criticism and failure. I felt frightened to bring my otherness to the fore and I didn't realise it was my otherness that bound all the parts of my identity.

I wondered for a long time where this fear came from. There were lots of instances in my youth where I put something out into the world and it wasn't received the way I'd intended. Design thinking helped me to identify and address those feelings and experiences, to be aware of when my inner critic is speaking up or when a trigger is causing me to breathe tighter and make my temper boil. It has taught me to consider things not going to plan as learnings, not failures, and to reframe and retest.

I once did a personality test. The facilitator called me over and told me that my result was unique in the group of twenty-five. She explained that most people either like to do things quickly or like to do them right. She told me I felt compelled to do them quickly and to do them correctly. It was one of the most liberating things anyone had ever told me. The facilitator also told me that my results were the same in a calm state and in a conflicted or stressed state.

'You must handle stress really well,' she said. 'Your responses didn't change from one state to the other.'

'Or I'm just always in a state of conflict or stress,' I responded.

I am still working on how I put myself out into the world. I'm learning not to take things personally and to avoid defensiveness. I am always growing through that process despite being fired, being made redundant and leaving jobs that were toxic. I undertook emotional intelligence training and learned that I can be impulsive in my responses and too direct when I feel my values are threatened. This, of course, affects how others perceive me. I have learned that stepping down or walking away doesn't mean failure. I have learned that coming back to my own essence requires curiosity, bravery, vulnerability and compassion. It required me to dig deep into my otherness and the things that make me whole.

I have reflected deeply on what leadership means to me as part of the prototyping process. I have always been self-motivated. When I worked in a group, I often took charge, particularly because I wanted to do well and trusted my own capabilities, but also because I didn't trust that others could do it as well as me.

One of the challenges is that there are few women leaders who are brave and vulnerable enough to publicly say that they're struggling, spent, and can't continue on the same path, whether personal or professional. They know that their vision for themselves won't come true, but they are okay with that. Every decision has a cost and success and meaning are not the same. Sharing real, honest and raw stories allows us to develop a different notion of success, one with an internal rather than external barometer, one of meaning rather than accolade.

The positive benefits of women telling their own stories can't be underestimated. The importance of women's voices and their absence has been a crucial learning from my journey. We need the voices of relatable peers to tell their stories. The stories of prominent women in public life are important and inspirational, but we normally don't see them talk about the day-to-day challenges of how they got to where they are. We see them once they have adult children and are at the top of their game.

Women need to hear the stories of successful women and what they sacrificed to get there. Being vulnerable about what leadership means and costs is important. We need to talk, too, about the role of men.[2] Many of the female leaders I look up to have acknowledged that their choice of life partner has been the defining feature in their success – sharing care responsibilities, taking turns at putting their careers on hold and contributing resources in an equitable way.

It was with men that I found vulnerability most challenging. For most of my life, I couldn't be vulnerable in my relationships. I protected myself, holding people to the standard by which I wanted to be treated. I wanted to be understood and wanted connection and meaning, not focusing on intellect but on emotions. I have never really been on my own, but I have definitely been lonely, isolated, unconnected and lacking meaning. I needed to find a way to be comfortable with my own company. I needed to put myself at the centre of my own story. I no longer wanted to be in a position where my emotional state was dependent on my partner. I needed to temper myself, measure myself, calm myself and make myself content. For me, by me.

I know my triggers and tipping points and have held the mirror

[2] King, Jackie. "She Speaks." Accessed 2018. http://www.womenaustralia. info/exhib/shespeaks/entry-jackie-king.html.

up to myself repeatedly. I've discovered how to be with and care for myself, back myself, let go when someone or something is bad for me (even if I don't want to), be happy and sad at the same time, and balance those emotions. In her book *Bittersweet*, Susan Cain equates sadness with empathy and caring, epitomised by compassion: '…we can turn pain into creativity. And that in turn can be rewarding by turning it into purpose and connection, meaning.'[3]

This is also relevant to vulnerable parenting. Being vulnerable as a mother is so hard, and arguably even more so as a single mother. It's difficult to be open to learning from your kids, accepting their different views, making changes because of their perceptions, altering your behaviours, responses, actions, guidance and influence. This kind of vulnerable parenting means I treat my kids as part of a community and team where they must also be vulnerable and true to themselves, deal with things that they don't want to and solve problems together.

I show my kids that I have to make tough choices, believe in myself and look after myself to be my best self for them. I breathe differently now; I have had a transformational change. I carve out time for myself to meditate, do yoga and walk the dog. My voice is lower and calmer. My language is simpler yet, at the same time, less absolute or extreme. I am not trying to impress them or be their friend. I know my worth.

At various moments, we all find solace in our children. There is nothing better than a cuddle on the couch at the end of the day, a walk around the park talking about their lives or issues, or reading together in bed. They nourish us as much as we support them.

---

[3]   Cain, Susan. *Bittersweet: How Sorrow and Longing Make Us Whole*. New York: Random House, 2022.

Many women are happy spending time with their children as a replacement for a present husband or loving partner. However, I think it is dangerous to expect our children to be able to provide us with the sense of belonging that we should be receiving from adult relationships. Eventually, they will grow up and leave, and our whole sense of self could be left without a base, without a reference point. And then what? From my diary:

> *We give, we sacrifice and compromise, we live through and for our children. And they know it. And they should know it. Jewish mothers are especially notorious for helicopter parenting, making children feel guilty, and checking they have eaten enough, are mixing with the right people, and are on a path to success. But as the product of a Jewish mother, and now the mother of Jewish products, and having sat on both sides of the fence – the receiver and the giver – I just want my kids to know I have their back. Always. That they belong. I will always be there for them, even when they aren't there for me. That's it.*

Prototype: A work in progress

When developing various prototypes, it is important to recognise that this is a lifelong journey. Health conditions, world events and things outside your control will challenge your sense of self. It is a work in progress.

To begin this process, ask:

- What can I do for my own self-care?
- What do I want to focus on? What can I manage? What is realistic right now?
- How can I be more vulnerable
  - in leadership,
  - at work,
  - in my relationships, and
  - in my parenting?

TEST AND LAUNCH

Once you know how you want to put yourself out into the world, you need to test it in the market. What impact does it have? How does it help or hinder you? What else can you learn about yourself and how others perceive you? This is an opportunity to gather further knowledge about yourself. The learnings obtained in this stage can be used to redefine problems and to modify and refine yourself in a circular process.

Over many years, I tested myself in different contexts, with different lenses. Most recently, it has been with a Jewish lens. What am I prepared to put out into the world in relation to my Jewishness? How do I balance my innate desire to advocate and tell the world about rising antisemitism, silence in relation to the rape of Israeli women and the confronting experiences of Jewish students on campus? How do I have a voice in the room to positively influence decision-making? To avoid regressing to my old exhausted, baggy-eyed person, I need to take care of myself, control my stress and not feel incongruent. I had gone through a journey of awareness of my values so that I could understand when they were being threatened. I understood better how my values evolved and how they manifested in certain behaviours.

At the end of the day, I only have myself to account to and live with. I look at how far I have come, detangling my past and dealing with things I have avoided for a long time. I have slowly rediscovered myself, my essence, the original me, and morphed into the future me, the independent, vulnerable, whole me I want to be, without the inner critic dominating. I am at one with my otherness.

I read about inspiring women, some of whom I know, and all they have achieved. They are brilliant and influential, but often, what we see is only half a story. We rarely see the reality of how they got there, their struggles, their compromises and the costs they bore. The reality of women's experiences is as important a part of the narrative as the successes.

Storytelling is how we give our lives a pathway. It helps me test my vulnerability. Writing this book over many years and iterations has helped launch a new version of me.

From my diary:

> *I feel so at peace when I write, so congruent within myself, so authentic. Perhaps my need to write is telling me that I need to stare out of the window, or that rather than reaching out to others in my writing and my story, the act of writing is in fact what is connecting me to others – the writer who is bubbling to get a story out that is trapped within. Maybe all my writing was merely seeking to understand myself. Maybe it was*

a means, a creative outlet that I was desperate for at a time when I had no other options. My emotional cup was full. This was the only thing that made me feel better. I always thought that it was about what I wrote, but rather, it was about the process of connecting and understanding myself, giving my-self a vulnerable narrative.

And then there are the things you need to deal with that you can't control, as you confront your own mortality. From my diary:

Your oxygen is low, you aren't allowed to move, use the phone, go to the toilet – we have called an ambulance. You have a massive clot in your lungs very close to an artery. You are a huge risk for a pulmonary embolism. What would happen to my kids without me? It happens more than we think. Women who push their own medical needs to the bottom of the priori-ty list. Women who ignore little pains and discomfort because they don't have time to make the appointment or look after themselves.

The world was telling me to stay small. To be still. To listen to my inner narrative and my body. To step back and make sure I didn't run out of breath. And then the problem I needed to solve changed again. I needed to start again… with empathy.

Learnings Not Failures

The design process is iterative – it needs continual testing, as you launch different options with different people and in different contexts across every domain of your life.

To begin this process, ask:

- How do I put myself out there?
- What should I try?
- What do I say to myself? To others?
- What worked and what didn't? Why?
- What can I keep as a new practice?
- What do I need to change?
- What else is missing?
- What else can I try?

THE ULTIMATE OTHER

I am trying as best I can to live in the now, not in the past. I am living with myself in the most authentic and vulnerable way I can. And I write. But as I think about the next iteration of myself, and the role that storytelling and writing have played in the context of design thinking, I wonder how we can design our own futures, systems and institutions.

I have shared my reflections as I applied design thinking to the process of finding myself and emerging as an independent, vulnerable woman. But I'm not at the end of the journey. World events and my health also tell me that I'm not there yet.

For months, I was frozen trying to figure out how to integrate my shifting identity as a Jew into this book. I couldn't even begin to understand my internal narrative. I just stopped. The images of those women and girls in captivity or dead, with blood-stained pants, having been violated and mutilated in the most barbaric ways, kept me up at night. I was on the verge of tears all the time. I felt a transcendence, living both in my past and my present – a surreal existentialism as I watched and experienced the world and, at the same time, felt all the assumptions I had made about my place in it turn on their heads. It defied logic and civility.

And that's the beautiful thing about the approach in this book. There are no time restrictions. It's okay to stop and breathe. To listen to your inner thoughts, to understand yourself and the world around you. To connect to your past, to earlier versions of yourself, to your past experiences and your past generations. To be empathetic about the decisions you have made and your contributions, even if there is no longer a place for you there. Even if you need to recreate yourself professionally or leave an environment where you no longer feel you can be authentic or vulnerable.

I'm practising empathy for myself. Asking the right questions, testing, iterating, starting again. Redesigning my life. Being comfortable and self-actualising my otherness. Woman. Divorced. Jew.

AND THE CYCLE REPEATS

When I look over all the things I have tried over the last two decades to help me move forwards across all the spheres of my life, I can summarise them across the process of design thinking. They are not linear stages – they can occur simultaneously, and one stage doesn't need to be completed before moving on to the next.

Empathise

Ask yourself:

What are my values? How do I understand and work towards meaning in my life? What are my needs and desires? Why are they important to me? What is my vision for myself and what is my inner critic telling me? How does it hold me back? What does it mean to be a single mother and a woman of a certain age in today's world? What relationships are working for me and which ones do I need to let go of? How do I practise self compassion and resilience? What can I change?

The following approaches helped me learn about my inner critic and understand myself with self-compassion:

- I undertook various therapies to understand the end of my marriage, my triggers, intergenerational trauma, and my relationships with my parents, grandparents and men.
- I dug deep to understand and articulate my values.
- I started to develop and craft a narrative about myself and where I held myself back.
- I was kinder to myself and tried not to feel the pressure to succeed and surpass.
- I stepped off boards and away from organisations and people that made me feel inauthentic.
- I began to see failure as learning.
- I spent time alone.
- I learned how to breathe.
- I read books about the Holocaust, antisemitism, Jewish identity, social cohesion and gender.
- I understood how trauma manifested in my physicality and my relationship to food.

Define

Ask yourself:

How do I put myself out into the world? How does the world perceive me? What are the different versions of me that I want to focus on? Where and when have I felt my most authentic self? What parts of my identity am I uncomfortable with? What am I reluctant to share with others? When have I felt alone or different? How might my various identities align in a narrative?

The following actions helped me understand the problem I wanted to solve:

- I sat in my Jewishness.
- I cried for Jews everywhere.
- I came to terms with my feminism and the reality of the women's rights movement.
- I supported my children to become resilient, self-confident and independent.
- I became financially literate.
- I undertook an EMBA and explored professional and personal development via emotional intelligence, leadership courses, management courses, women in leadership, academic leadership, decision-making, data and leadership.
- I took on a range of different jobs and consultancies to understand how the market perceived me.
- I decided to bring my whole self to all that I do.

Ideate

Ask yourself:
What would I do with my finances, in my career, my relationships, my physicality, my religion, my cultural interests and my creative being if time and money were not considerations? How do I want to establish and maintain my independence? What am I most proud of? What do I regret or feel shame for? What do I want to learn? How do I want to grow?

In this ideation process I focused on the following:

- I learned how to become independent, financially and emotionally.

- I invested my time in the arts and literature.
- I reflected on the times in my life that gave me the most joy and pride.
- I applied for jobs, aiming for a higher level with each career move.
- I managed my team the way I wanted to be managed, with trust, psychological safety and flexibility.
- I stopped trying to be right.
- I stopped trying to compete.
- I stopped trying to be everything to everyone.
- I increasingly understood the way my communications and responses affected those around me.
- I mentored a range of people, supporting them and learning about myself in the process.

Prototype

Ask yourself:
How do I care for myself emotionally and physically? What do I want to focus on? What can I manage? What is realistic and affordable right now? How can I be more vulnerable in leadership, at work, in my relationships and in my parenting?

As part of my prototyping process, I tried the following strategies:

- I started with things that didn't cost much money to improve my self-care – healthier eating, walking, yoga and meditating.
- I continued to spend time in the arts and literature, finding moments of joy in those spaces.

- I tried to be more vulnerable in all my relationships.
- I investigated and started dealing with my health issues.

Test and launch

Ask yourself:
What did I try? What worked and what didn't? Why? What was my internal narrative during this time? How did I put myself out into the world? What can I keep as a new practice? What do I still need to change? What did I learn?

As part of the testing process, I came to terms with the reality of failure, and things not working out the way I had planned. I had many doomed relationships, arguments with my parents and children, stress, illness, exhaustion and failures at work. But I became more comfortable in my otherness, in my independence and in my vulnerability.

During this phase:

- I was curious – I started asking questions of myself and my children, and questioning my assumptions about the world.
- I accepted that relaxation and exercise were constructive uses of my time.
- I focused on contentedness rather than happiness.
- I asked for help.
- I wrote and wrote and wrote.
- I chose me.

And the cycle starts again…

BIBLIOGRAPHY

de Botton, A. (2020) *School of Life: An Emotional Education* (Penguin Books: UK)

Bolick, K. (2016) *Spinster: Making a Life of One's Own* (Little Brown: UK)

Brown, B. (2018) *Dare to Lead* (Vermilion: London)

Burnett, B. and Evans, D. (2016) *Designing Your Life: How to Build a Well-Lived, Joyful Life* (Random House: UK)

Cain, S. (2022) *Bittersweet: How Sorrow and Longing Make Us Whole* (Crown Publishing Group: UK)

Cross, R. and Dillon, K. (2023) 'The Hidden Toll of Microstress', *Harvard Business Review* at https://hbr.org/2023/02/the-hidden-toll-of-microstress

Cuddy, A. (2015) *Presence: Bringing your Boldest Self to Your Biggest Challenges* (Orion: GB)

Delizonna, L. (2017) 'High Performing Teams Need Psychological Safety' *Harvard Business Review* at https://hbr.org/2017/08/high-performing-teams-need-psychological-safety-heres-how-to-create-it

Doyle, G. (2020) *Untamed* (Random House: UK)

Duckworth, A. (2016) *Grit: The Power of Passion and Perseverance* (Random House: UK)

Esfahani Smith, E. (2017) *The Power of Meaning: The True Route to Happiness* (Random House: UK)

Fox, C. (2018) 'Busting the Merit Myth', *Australian Institute of Company Directors* at https://www.aicd.com.au/board-of-directors/diversity/gender/busting-the-merit-myth.html

Fox, C. (2009)'"Hits and Myths About Reaching the Upper Ranks', *Australian Financial Review* at https://www.afr.com/companies/hits-and-myths-about-reaching-the-upper-ranks-20091027-iwj1u

Frei, F. X. and Morriss, A. (2020) 'Begin with Trust: The First Step to Becoming a Genuinely Empowering Leader' *Harvard Business Review* at https://hbr.org/2020/05/begin-with-trust

Gladwell, M. (2009) *Outliers* (Penguin Books: UK)

Goleman, D. (2021) *Emotional Intelligence: Why It Can Matter More Than IQ* (Bloomsbury Publishing: US)

Grant, A. (2021) *Think Again: The Power of Knowing What You Don't Know* (Random House: UK)

Grant, A. (2017) *Originals: How Non-Conformists Change the World* (Random House: UK)

Huffington, A. (2015) *Thrive: The Third Metric to Redefining Success and Creating a Life of Well Being, Wisdom, and Wonder* (Harmony Books: US)

Ibarra. H. (2004) *Working Identity: Unconventional Strategies for Reinventing Your Career* (Harvard Business Review Press: US)

Jaku, E. (2020) *The Happiest Man on Earth* (Pan Macmillan Australia: Australia)

Kahneman, D. (2011) *Thinking, Fast and Slow* (Farrar, Straus & Giroux Inc.: US)

King, J. (2018) *She Speaks* at http://www.womenaustralia.info/exhib/shespeaks/entry-jackie-king.html

Klinenberg, E. (2012) *Going Solo: The Extraordinary Rise and Surprising Appeal of Living Alone* (Duckworth Books: UK)

Lepore, J. (2020) 'The History of Loneliness', *The New Yorker* at https://www.newyorker.com/magazine/2020/04/06/the-history-of-loneliness

Maisel, E. (2012) '"The Smart Gap: How to deal with painful shortfalls in brainpower' *Psychology Today* at https://www.psychologytoday.com/intl/blog/rethinking-mental-health/201204/the-smart-gap

Martin, W. (2016) *Primates of Park Avenue: A Memoir* (Simon and Schuster: US)

Pink, D. (2018) *Drive: The Surprising Truth About What Motivates Us* (A&U Canongate: GB)

Pinsker, J. (2016) 'Why So Many Smart People Aren't Happy', *The Atlantic* at https://www.theatlantic.com/business/archive/2016/04/why-so-many-smart-people-arent-happy/479832/

Putnam, R. D. (2020) *Bowling Alone: The Collapse and Revival of American Community* (Simon and Schuster: US)

Sandberg, S. (2015) *Lean In: Women, Work, and the Will to Lead* (Random House: UK)

Schamer, O. (2016) *Theory U: Leading from the Future as it Emerges* (Berrett-Koehler Publishers: US)

Slaughter, A.M. (2016) *Unfinished Business: Women Men Work Family* (One World Publications: GB)

Solomon, A. (2014) *Far from the Tree: Parents, Children, and the Search for Identity* (Random House: UK)

Theroux, A. (2021) *The Year of the End: A Memoir of Marriage, Truth, and Fiction* (Icon Books: UK)

Tippet, K. (2018) *Becoming Wise: An Inquiry into the Mystery and Art of Living* (Little Brown: UK)

Van der Kolk, B. (2014) *The Body Keeps the Score: Brain, Mind and Body in the Healing of Trauma* (Penguin Books: UK)

Waldman, A. (2010) *Bad Mother: A Chronicle of Maternal Crimes, Minor Calamities and Occasional Moments of Grace* (Random House: US)

Westervelt, A. (2018) *Forget 'Having It All': How America Messed Up Motherhood – and How to Fix It* (Seal Press: US)

Wittenberg-Cox, A. (2017) 'If You Can't Find a Spouse Who Supports Your Career, Stay Single', *Harvard Business Review* at https://hbr.org/2017/10/if-you-cant-find-a-spouse-who-supports-your-career-stay-single

Woolf, V. (2009) *A Room of One's Own* (Penguin Books: UK)

ABOUT THE AUTHOR

D r Jackie King has over twenty years of experience in consulting in the for-purpose sector. She has written and self-published two children's books, as well as many academic and media articles on issues relating to community development, refugee policy and gender. A lawyer by training, she completed a PhD in refugee policy and an EMBA in leadership and strategy. Jackie is an advocate of design thinking as a tool for creating impact and change. Her first experiment with design thinking was a women's capacity-building program, Project Deborah, for professional women who were generally underutilised and undervalued in their communities. Jackie designed the program with the participants as beneficiaries, asking them what they needed to fulfil their own ambitions and accelerate their growth and development. Jackie took the learnings from running this program to apply the principles of design thinking in her own life after the end of her marriage. She is passionate about storytelling and believes in the value of sharing stories to connect people and build empathy.